TRICERATOPS

By Daisy Allyn

Gareth Stevens
PUBLISHING

leveled reader
science

Please visit our website, www.garethstevens.com. For a free color catalog of all our high-quality books, call toll free 1-800-542-2595 or fax 1-877-542-2596.

Library of Congress Cataloging-in-Publication Data

Allyn, Daisy.
Triceratops / by Daisy Allyn.
p. cm. — (A look at dinosaurs)
Includes index.
ISBN 978-1-4824-1831-6 (pbk.)
ISBN 978-1-4824-1829-3 (6-pack)
ISBN 978-1-4824-1830-9 (library binding)
1. Triceratops — Juvenile literature. I. Allyn, Daisy. II. Title.
QE862.O65 A45 2015
567.9158—d23

Published in 2015 by
Gareth Stevens Publishing
111 East 14th Street, Suite 349
New York, NY 10003

Designer: Nicholas Domiano
Editor: Ryan Nagelhout

Illustrations by Jeffrey Mangiat
Science Consultant: Philip J. Currie, Ph.D., Professor and Canada Research Chair of Dinosaur Palaeobiology at the University of Alberta, Canada

Printed in the United States of America

CPSIA compliance information: Batch #CW15GS: For further information contact Gareth Stevens, New York, New York at 1-800-542-2595.

Contents

Boldface words appear in the glossary.

A Three-Horned Face

Dinosaurs lived millions of years ago. There were many kinds of dinosaurs. One dinosaur walked on four legs and had horns on its head. It was the *Triceratops* (try-SEHR-uh-tahps). This name means "three-horned face."

Dinosaur Defenses

The *Triceratops*'s horns were very important. They helped guard the *Triceratops* against other dinosaurs, such as the *Tyrannosaurus rex*. A *Triceratops* **defended** itself by running toward a *Tyrannosaurus rex* with its sharp horns.

What's a Frill?

The *Triceratops* is known for its three horns. But that wasn't the only cool thing on its head. It also had a **frill**. Scientists think the frill guarded the *Triceratops* from other dinosaurs' **attacks**. It might have helped the *Triceratops* find a **mate**, too.

9

A Big Body

Now that you know about the *Triceratops*'s head, let's learn about its body. It was huge! The *Triceratops* was 30 feet (9 m) long. That's about as long as two cars. The *Triceratops* was also very heavy, weighing about as much as three cars.

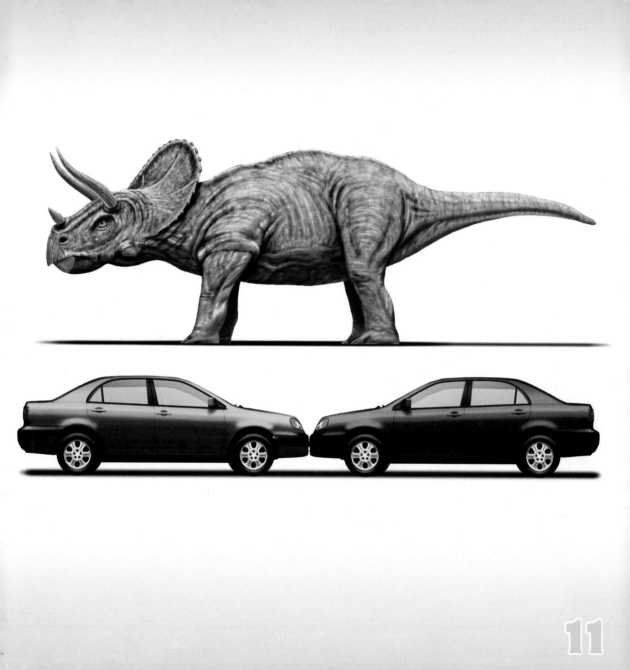

Slow and Steady

Some dinosaurs moved quickly, but probably not the *Triceratops*. It was too heavy! The *Triceratops*'s four short legs carried its body weight. They weren't made to move fast. But the *Triceratops* could still run faster than humans.

13

Thick-Skinned

The *Triceratops* had thick skin, but the skin probably wasn't very hard. How do we know? Many *Triceratops* **fossils** have holes in them. The holes may be from other dinosaurs' bites or attacks. They cut through the skin, all the way to the bone!

15

Plant Eater

The *Triceratops* ate plants. Its beaklike mouth and sharp teeth were perfect for chewing leaves and branches. Since the *Triceratops* was short, it ate plants that grew low to the ground. It needed a lot of food to keep its big body going.

Alone and in Groups

Nobody knows if the *Triceratops* lived alone or in groups called herds. Scientists usually find *Triceratops* fossils by themselves. But they have also found fossils of many *Triceratops* together. They think young *Triceratops* traveled in herds to stay safe.

19

Dinosaur Bones

How do we know so much about the *Triceratops*? We've learned about them by studying fossils. Some **museums** have complete sets of *Triceratops* fossils for people to see. They even have full models of what their bodies might have looked like!

TRICERATOPS

21

Glossary

attack: an attempt to harm someone or something

defend: to guard against harm

fossil: the hardened remains of an animal or plant that lived long ago

frill: a strip of bone with a curved edge that grows out of a creature's neck

mate: one of two animals that come together to produce babies

museum: a building in which things of interest are displayed

For More Information

Books

Dixon, Dougal. *Everything You Need to Know About Dinosaurs*. New York, NY: Kingfisher, 2012.

Dodson, Peter. *Triceratops Up Close: Horned Dinosaur*. Berkeley Heights, NJ: Enslow Publishers, 2011.

Websites

Dinosaurs—Triceratops
kids-dinosaurs.com/dinosaurs-triceratops.html
Visit this website to learn more about the *Triceratops*.

Walking with Dinosaurs: Triceratops
walkingwithdinosaurs.com/dinosaurs/detail/triceratops/
The British Broadcasting Company's website for the movie *Walking with Dinosaurs* teaches cool facts about the *Triceratops* and other dinosaurs.

Publisher's note to educators and parents: Our editors have carefully reviewed these websites to ensure that they are suitable for students. Many websites change frequently, however, and we cannot guarantee that a site's future contents will continue to meet our high standards of quality and educational value. Be advised that students should be closely supervised whenever they access the Internet.

Index